D1796434

A MAD POET'S RAMBLINGS

BY POETIC VERSE I'M LED
BOOK 1

ROBERT WORRALL
(A MAD POET)

DEDICATION

I dedicate this book to all those people of the past who have walked and trekked around this isle.

I ramble this isle
this poetic scene,
looking for the places
I've not, yet been.

Robert Worrall

CONTENTS

A Mad Poet's Ramblings

ACKNOWLEDGMENTS

I wish to thank all the places I have visited in this book for giving me the
inspirations I need to write these poems.
I would also like to thank them for allowing me to ramble around such
beautiful and amazing places.

Notes

Enter Inside

Enter pages
of a secret domain,
ramble round,
on natures plain.

deep inside
the verse of leaves
enter the mind
your vision, perceives.

Drawn within
these pages bound
you'll see the places
that will, astound.

See the past
ancient and prime,
feel it now,
in a poem, a rhyme.

Read my words,
of the places surreal
your mind's inside,
words, you feel.

Deep within
by verse you're led
photos to see,
poetry, to be read.

Sandbach Crosses

Standing in a market place
proud and tall
ignored by the many
but a few, hear their call.

Lots of people pass
while shopping each day
yet very few care
for the megaliths, in decay.

Two Saxon crosses
a mysterious work of art
that back in the past
were smashed, broke apart.

Their pieces scattered
all over the land
brought back together
and reassembled, to stand.

In Sandbach town
are these crosses to adore
they're carved so skilfully,
and hold tales, galore.

The next you pass
remember, they're there
the crosses are silent
yet they see you, and stare.

Sandbach Crosses.

Opposite side of Sandbach Crosses.

Robert Worrall

Westbury White Horse

On the edge of Bratton Downs
a white horse stands still
it's the white horse of Westbury
the horse, on the hill.

It's the oldest horse in Wiltshire
over lands it does survey,
yet another was originally here
that faced, the other way.

It's the belief that you honour
a victory by the great
the greatest King, King Alfred
a yarn, to celebrate.

Your outline has changed
and vandals have done you harm
yet still you survive
it's another story, to your charm.

You've seen so much in history
been illuminated by light
the last time a Diamond Jubilee
for Queen, standing bright.

On the edge of Bratton Downs
a white horse stands still
it's the white horse of Bratton
you're stunning, you're brill.

Westbury White Horse keeping watch.

Westbury White Horse viewed from the road below.

Castle of Grandeur

Beside the river Avon
is a castle, of stone
originally built by William
the Conqueror, well known.

During the hundred year war
stone replaced the wood
now it's medieval
it's a stronghold, still good.

Queen Victoria has visited
in eighteen fifty eight
come to see the fourth Earl
celebrations, were great.

I walked around this castle
this castle, so grand
today it's still magnificent
and certainly, in demand.

This castle is so beautiful
with its legends and ghosts
it's a wonderful place to visit
for the history, it boasts.

Beside the River Avon
Warwick Castle, stands tall
today it's still amazing
with lots of tales, to enthral.

View of Warwick Castle from the mound.

View of the Chapel, Great Hall and State Rooms.

West Kennet Long Barrow

West Kennet Long Barrow
a Neolithic chambered tomb
one of Britain's largest
an ancient, deathly, womb.

Walk around the outside
behold a monument so vast
sense and feel it's draw
it's the ancient, it's the past.

You're taken in by its beauty
with its stones so large
as you're drawn to the front
the ancients, take charge.

Enter into the darkness
the underworld deep below
enter into the silence
that eerie stillness, of woe.

As you walk into the passage
you sense a life of the past
feeling down its walls
your emotions, are surpassed.

The silence and stillness
bring an eerie peace, of mind
you know something's missing
a conundrum, of humankind.

Front view of West Kennet Long Barrow

View of the stones inside.

Greyfriars Cloisters

Greyfriars Cloisters
near the historic quay
completely in ruins
it's a sight, to see.

Greyfriars Cloisters
not much to see
Franciscan monks
grey friars, they be.

Greyfriars Cloisters
an eerie place
laid bare by bombs
wartime, disgrace.

Greyfriars Cloisters
of 13th Century
your charm has gone
you're now, eerie.

Greyfriars Cloisters
Gt. Yarmouth you be
ruined and alone
the railings, hide thee.

Greyfriars Cloisters
once so proud
now you're empty
no prayers, allowed.

Greyfriars Cloisters from the footpath.

Seofan Beorgas

The seven barrows
Seofan Beorgas
rounded mounds
covered, in grass.

Near to Avebury
where they reside
from the Bronze Age,
it's a rough guide.

Overton Hill
is the sacred place
a haunt of the past
an ancient, race.

An unknown mystery
of a time long gone
ancient burials
forgotten, overrun.

Why was it sacred?
What did they mean?
No one knows
it's quiet, it's serene.

Overton Hill
their last resting place
ancient peoples
of a forgotten, race.

Close up of one of the barrows.

Three of the barrows in a line.

Hiding in the Woods

Hiding deep in the woods
with birds and bees
lies a beautiful castle ruin
all shrouded, by trees.

Walk the path of nature
to a relic of the past
Ewloe Castle, Wales
shall leave you, aghast.

A 13th Century castle
to honour a victory brief
a victory of Llywelyn
a Welsh Prince, and chief.

By twelve seventy seven
it's a castle deserted
Edward the first's invasion
could not, be averted.

It now lies in ruins
a hidden memorial of old
a Welsh castle empty
to which I, have strolled.

It's hiding in those woods
waiting for you, to find
a beautiful dreamy land
with a memorial, enshrined.

View near the entrance of Ewloe Castle.

View of the castle peeking through the trees.

Lyme Park

Disley is the town
and Lyme Park the place
it's a beautiful mansion
so grand, it's ace.

Dated to the 16th Century
home of the Leghs
given to the National Trust
in 1946, were the keys.

Enter into the house
and revisit a time long gone
take the guided tour
and get more, information.

Walk around the gardens
or the outer grounds
watch out for the deer
and listen, to the sounds.

Stroll out to the belvedere
the Lantern, it's name
a really weird monument
for the scenic, frame.

Don't forget the Cage
the hunting lodge up high
we need more days
but for now, it's goodbye.

View of Lyme Park from across the lake.

The Cage.

Ladies of the Past

Edwardian ladies
you're dressed in style
when I looked your way
you gave, a smile.

I watched you walk
in Lyme Park grounds
two lovely ladies
in beautiful, surrounds.

Dressed in clothes
neither dull, nor bright
you're still so vibrant
and really, polite.

Everyone watches
while you walk on past
I can see their faces
with their eyes, aghast.

You look so simple
in those dresses so plain
yet you're also stunning
I can't, explain.

Edwardian ladies
you're a pleasure to see
you gave us insight
from our past, history.

The Edwardian Ladies at Lyme Park.

Chalice Well

Oh Chalice Well,
you're a healing well
serene and quiet
I'm under, your spell.

Oh Chalice Well
aside Glastonbury Tor
a sacred space
that we all, can adore.

Oh Chalice Well
with gardens around
the essence of life
you do, astound.

Oh Chalice Well
your waters run free
you are amazing
you're pure, energy.

Oh Chalice Well
with your reddish hue
the waters never stop
you always, spew.

Oh Chalice Well
where the waters flow
a treasure to seek
for your spirit, to grow.

One of the features in Chalice Well Gardens

Home of a Baron

Corsham Court
the Methuen family seat,
a wonderful place
for a Baron, to meet.

Surrounded by a park
a Capability Brown design
'tis a wonderful place
for a poet, to define.

Part of a queen's dower
in the days of old
for Catherine of Aragon
once, controlled.

I travelled to this place
sadly it was closed,
I took a few photos
through gates, I nosed.

I stood and gazed
at this magnificent court
this historical place
with nothing, to report.

Like a peasant of the land
I stared in awe
at this wonderful manor
I couldn't, explore.

Photo of Corsham Court from the gate.

Photo from outside the gate.

Silence

I walked into the grounds
of an abbey in bits
even though it's a ruin
a sense of grandeur, emits.

Founded in the 7th century
a monastery so grand,
suppressed by a King
and the last abbot, hanged.

It's a place full of history
linked to the grail
and associations too
with King Arthur's, fairytale.

I looked all around me
at these ruins standing out
so peaceful and quiet
with a sense, of the devout.

You walk in amazement
and try to envision the past
now what was it like?
for those monks, harassed.

Glastonbury Abbey
a sacred place now in decay
a monastery without monks
in silence, it shall pray.

Glastonbury Abbey Ruins

The Lady Chapel

The Stones Speak

I went to a village
surrounded by stone
a Neolithic monument
a mystery, unknown.

I walked the paths
by stones standing high
three stone circles
within a henge, I sigh.

Peace and tranquility
the mystery of ago
it's a wonderful setting
for a spirit, to glow.

I sense something
as time's standing still
the stones speak
I can hear, their shrill.

Cries from the past
the voices of the dead
the circles are alive
by these stones, I'm led.

Avebury's the place
where stones converse
listen to the voices
hear the winds, of verse.

Avebury Stone Circle

Avebury Manor

Wilton Church

On West Street in Wilton
a church stands tall
St. Mary and St. Nicholas
to you, will call.

A building masterpiece
to replace the old
a Victorian marvel
standing proud, and bold.

You will not miss it
it's magnificence shines
you can't ignore it
Romanesque, designs.

This tiny little town
with an enormous church
makes you want to enter
for more, research.

You're drawn to the tower
where bells reside
you stand in awe
with mouth, open wide.

When you walk inside
a stunning work of art hits
you can only admire
the magnificence, it emits.

Inside Wilton Church

Wilton Church from the roadside.

Tegg's Nose

Tegge's Naze, Tegge's Naze
such beauty, to amaze.
Tegge's Naze, Tegge's Naze
you're a place, to praise.

Tegge's Naze, Tegg's Nose
it's amazing, I suppose.
Tegge's Naze, Tegg's Nose
it's a gem, to expose.

Tegg's Nose, Tegg's Nose
a country park, arose.
Tegg's Nose, Tegg's Nose
rich in history, it shows.

Tegge's Naze, Tegge's Naze
with sheep, that graze.
Tegge's Naze, Tegge's Naze
past history, Bronze Age

Tegge's Naze, Tegg's Nose
have a walk, have a doze.
Tegge's Naze, Tegg's Nose
your story, you compose.

Tegge's Naze, Tegge's Naze
a beautiful place, to amaze
Tegg's Nose, Tegg's Nose
with its scenery, that glows.

View of Tegg's Nose and Bottoms Reservoirs.

Tegg's Nose old quarry machinery.

The Castle of Tears

Home of the Hungerfords
for 300 years
this castle in ruin
has witnessed, many tears.

A castle extended
by a Knight of the Garter
the first Lord Hungerford
with, Royal Charter.

In the War of the Roses
death overflows
the last Lord Hungerford
killed, by white rose.

Sold in sixteen eighty six
to repay his debts
the last of the Hungerfords
had no, regrets.

It's a castle full of intrigue,
scandal and misery
it's a castle in ruins
without, any war history.

I took in the sites
of this castle rich in tales
looking at the coffins
strange, anthropoid, details.

Farleigh Hungerford Castle.

The Anthropoid Coffins.

Lytes Cary Manor

By Charlton Mackrell
in Somerset,
is Lytes Cary Manor
a Botanists, epithet.

With a creative garden
arts and crafts style
this place is a dream
that'll make you, smile.

I walked the gardens
and followed the trails
where Lytes and Jenners
had told, their tales.

I toured the chapel
the oldest surviving part
it's quiet, it's silent
it's quaint, and it's smart.

Made of blue lias stone
a house with appeal
the interior is stunning
it's artistic, surreal.

Lytes Cary Manor
a complete work of art,
inside and outside
a creation, of the heart.

Lytes Cary Manor House.

View of Lytes Cary from the main road.

Glastonbury Tor

Off we went
to Glastonbury town
to visit the Tor
a place, of renown.

Off we walked
to the foot of the Tor
this conical hill
is a place, to adore.

Off we went
following the path
venturing up
we're having, a laugh.

Step by step
to the summit we go
looking around
at the lands, below.

Slowly, slowly
our minds at peace
summit reached
it's a magical, release.

We gaze at the tower
feeling renewed
the Tor has an energy
spirits, imbued.

Glastonbury Tor and St. Michael's Tower.

View from the top of the path.

Alnwick Castle

Alnwick Castle
is the seat of a Duke
his stately house
and home, to a spook.

Alnwick Castle
in its tunnels below
has a ghostly girl
the Grey Lady, of ago.

Alnwick Castle
was defeated and lost
King David the first
of Scotland, crossed.

Alnwick Castle
seen in film and show
like Harry Potter
and the film, Ivanhoe.

Alnwick Castle
has charm and appeal
yet in the past
it wasn't, genteel.

Alnwick Castle
with beauty all around
Ralph Percy, Duke
his castle, we've found.

Alnwick Castle.

Statue of Harry Hotspur.

St. Bart's Church, Corsham.

St. Bartholomews's Church
stands proud and tall
in the town of Corsham
where it does, enthral.

With its thinness of walls
and a nave so slender,
indicative of Saxon work
a church, of splendor.

In the Twelfth Century
they added a little more
aisles and a chancel
it's the Norman, decor.

A Lady Chapel did come
in the century after
but then it's rebuilt
many years, thereafter.

In the eighteen hundreds
the tower removed
to be replaced by another
I suppose, improved.

With all its history
from Saxon to present day
it's a beautiful church
take a peek, as you pray.

Inside St. Bart's Church

St. Bartholomews Church, Corsham.

Open and Bare

Lying open and bare
for all to view
forgotten ruins
an ancient, residue.

I pass the stones
weathered and worn
ghosts of the past
now, forlorn.

Many people lay here
buried long ago
Neolithic in time
it's a place, of woe.

I walk the aisle
as the sun does shine
amidst the stones
of an ancient, shrine.

Ancient memories
lying in the dust
lost in time
no more, discussed.

I visited a place
no tumulus, not whole
Nymphsfield barrow
no longer, a soul.

Nymphsfield Barrow.

Looking out from Nymphsfield Barrow.

Dyrham Park

Where once stood
a manor house
is Dyrham Park
the country house.

Beside a church
St. Peter's its name
of 13th Century
historic, acclaim.

Built for William
William Blathwayt
it's such a beautiful
country, estate.

View the house
or walk the grounds
see the deer
and Iron Age, mounds.

During the war
it became the home
for so many children
to safely, roam.

Dyrham Park
has many tales to tell
I took a peek
and fell under, its spell.

Dyrham Park.

View of Dyrham Park from the gardens.

Gawton's Stone

A hermit's home
Gorton Stone
in Greenway Bank
stands, alone.

Myth surrounds
a rock so large
this healing stone
feel, its charge.

A hermit once
fled to here
taken by plague
his life, in fear.

Gaze at the back
a face appears
features distinct
mystery, rears.

A burial place
menhir of stone,
forgotten statue
all, unknown.

Gorton's Dolmen
hides in view
it's a sacred place
built, by who?

The Face of Gawton's Stone.

Gawton's Stone.

Paxton House

Overlooking the Tweed
is a lovely house
built to woo
an heiress, to spouse.

It was a failed attempt
by Patrick Home
who left his heart
inside here, to roam.

Inside the house
is a gallery of fine art
Scottish related
they're really, smart.

Scotland's largest
Chippendale collection
in a beautiful setting
a house, of perfection.

Explore the grounds
the well and pond
it's woodland walks
and the river, beyond.

A children's playground
with a zip wire too
there's lots to see
and much more, to do.

Paxton House.

View from the woods behind Paxton House.

Lindisfarne

Crossing a causeway,
after high tide
I'm going to an island
that's sanctified.

Near to Scotland
the North East coast
Lindisfarne isle
St. Aidan, they boast.

Lindisfarne Priory
such a beautiful place
a priory in ruins
yet it's full, of grace.

The sun is shining
and the skies are blue
I feel at ease
by ancient, residue.

I can see the castle
in the distance up high
it's a glorious day
I've a tear, in my eye.

As I walk these ruins
the past I feel
you sense the prayers
on an isle, surreal.

Lindisfarne Priory.

Lindisfarne Castle

Past Glories

I trekked to a henge
on Marlborough Downs
to visit this site
of stones, with crowns.

The sun was shining
when I arrived
the day still young
yet visitors, thrived.

I gazed around
and admired the sight
of this ancient symbol
of power, alright.

It's a circle dismantled
past history lost
they're damaged stones
concrete, embossed.

Unlike any other,
stones from our history
this place is massive
a complete, mystery.

I felt really sad
for these stones now left
past glories gone
Stonehenge, is bereft.

Stonehenge in black and white

Stonehenge.

Home of the Guards

In the Scottish Borders
lies the town of Coldstream
home to the guards
with their band, supreme.

On the banks of the river
a quaint little town
with the oldest regiment
the guards, of renown.

I took a little peek
around this beautiful place
and found it delightful
so much history, to trace.

In Henderson Park
stands a memorial in stone
freedom of the Burgh
and a tercentenary, shown.

The day was wet and grey
when I visited here
yet still, it had lots to offer
this place, to endear.

One day I'll come back
to this curious little place
I loved every minute
with your history, to trace.

Freedom of the Burgh Stone in Henderson Park.

View of the bridge from Henderson Park.

Grinlow Tower

Sat high atop
on a Buxton hill
is Solomon's Temple
a folly, to thrill.

It's keeping watch
over the land,
high above
a place, so grand.

This sacred place
is a burial site
Bronze Age people
the Beaker, I cite.

A former structure
used to be here
by Solomon Mycock
a farmer, near.

Ninety two years
after it was erected
a 1988 restoration,
aided, the neglected.

Now once again
the temple is grand
guarding Grin Low
and it's sacred, land.

Grinlow Tower (Solomons Temple).

Close up of Solomons Temple.

Dough Cover

Dough Cover, Dough Cover
can you guess my name?
I'm near to Stonehenge
but without, it's fame.

Dough Cover, Dough Cover
a barrow once thought
then they realized
I'm a henge, distraught.

Dough Cover, Dough Cover
a henge that was wood
not much of me remains
my glories, misunderstood.

Dough Cover, Dough Cover
I'm so very, very, old
I'm marred by concrete
where posts, were holed.

Dough Cover, Dough Cover
I've six oval rings
long ago I was grand
now my heart, never sings.

Dough Cover, Dough Cover
can you guess my name?
they call me Woodhenge
a henge, deprived, of fame.

Dough Cover (Woodhenge), near the centre stone.

Dough Cover, (Woodhenge).

Robert Worrall

A Victorian Waterfall

Through these woods
and trees we go
listening to the birds
they're singing, "hello".

The rain has ended
the sun shines through
it's a beautiful place
in Teign Valley, it's true.

We reach the steps
and spot the waterfall
it's rocky terrain
so be careful, don't fall.

Ninety steps to go
the Buzzards view near
take it very slowly
take in the scenery, here.

We've reached halfway
in this beautiful land
not much further
to the peak, so grand.

I'm now at the top
and in the buzzards nest
it's magical up here
Canonteign, I'm impressed.

Canonteign woods and stream.

Canonteign Waterfall.

Longleat

Near to Warminster
is a stately home so fine
Elizabethan architecture
Rob Smythson, design.

Built for a Marquis
after a priory burnt down
an Augustinian priory
it's Longleat, of renown.

With thousands of acres
Capability Brown planned
it now has a safari park
that's become, in demand.

Built for the Thynnes
who today still reside here
the Marquis of Bath
a nobleman, and a peer.

The house itself
has a stunning Great Hall
with its minstrel's gallery
that's sure, to enthral.

Longleat House
the Marquis' stately home
so beautiful and historic
the perfect place, to roam.

Longleat House from the entrance.

Longleat House.

Cherhill White Horse

I'm the horse on the hill
just call me, Cherhill.
I'm the horse on the hill
I'm white, I'm still.

I was cut by a doctor
the mad doctor was he
who shouted his orders
by megaphone, hehe,

I've been here for ages
over 200 years
I'm getting too old
my coat, has smears.

I sit here and I watch
as the days go by
animals speak to me
and always say, "hi".

When first I was made
my eye was glass
and reflected the sun
as I lay, in the grass.

I'm the horse on the hill
just call me, Cherhill.
I'm the horse on the hill
I'm listening, but still.

Cherhill White Horse.

Cherhill White Horse in black and white.

Delamere Forest

I walked the forest
of Delamere
beside the trees
in nature's, sphere.

Forest of the lakes
Delamere means
a place of beauty
wonderful, scenes.

You're all that's left
of forests great
Mara and Mondrem,
you celebrate.

Blakemere Moss
now a lake restored
where wildlife thrives
nature, in accord.

Walk in the trees
as the Normans did
when hunting game
from animals, hid.

Listen to the sounds
of nature's bounty
in a beautiful forest
in a quiet, county.

Delamere Forest.

Blakemere Moss

Stoney Littleton

Stoney Littleton
is it a burial, or a shrine
peruse the outside
it's a mysterious, design.

Enter into the chamber
it's dark, as night
a little bit further
to a time, out of sight.

Touch the stones
and sense, past devotion
caress them slowly
overcome, by emotion.

The air is cold
as a breeze passes by
you wonder what it was
a mystery, you deny.

Keep on moving
till no more, can you go
trembling takes over
you sense, a hidden foe.

Scurrying back
to the light you can see
Stoney Littleton has
given you, it's mystery.

Stoney Littleton Long Barrow.

Looking out from inside.

Lacock Church

Lacock Church
St. Cyriac's by name
you're near to an abbey
an abbey, of fame.

Dedicated to St. Cyriac
a Norman saint
you're quite impressive
and very, quaint.

In the 14th Century
when your story began
then in the 15th
a rebuild, a new plan.

It gave you your shape
the shape of today
a perpendicular church
in a cruciform, way.

With so many changes
over the years
you still share prayers
hymns, and cheers.

Lacock Church
St. Cyriac's by name
such a beautiful church
in a place, of abbey fame.

Front view of Lacock Church.

Lacock Church, St. Cyriac's.

Totnes Castle

We stopped at this place
for something to eat
and noticed the castle
what a wonderful, treat.

It sits high atop a hill
looking down on the land
this motte and bailey
a Norman castle, is grand.

In the town of Totnes
this castle stands proud
it's position commanding
your senses, wowed.

We walked those steps
to the walls up high
it takes your breath away
literally, I sigh.

My daughter and I
tried to run up and down
to see how difficult it'd be
to attack, this mound.

It's a glorious castle
within a town on the Dart
I recommend it highly
it's a beautiful, work of art.

Totnes Castle.

Looking out from Totnes Castle.

Hanbury Pilgrim Cross

In a lonesome place
standing all alone
on a piece of grass
by a road, this stone.

A wayside marker
called Pilgrims Cross
an ancient symbol
that's now, at a loss.

This ancient cross
a forest path did mark
Feckenham Forest
no more trees, no bark.

The forest has gone
but it's marker stands
it's a cross to nowhere
no woods, no lands.

Silently pointing
it's a reminder of ago
an ancient cross
with a hidden, woe.

I stood by its side
as we got lost this day
it helped us out
and gave us, the way.

Hanbury Pilgrim Cross.

The sign next to the cross.

Babbacombe

We went to Babbacombe
to a clifftop green
we went to Babbacombe
it's quiet, and serene.

We went to Babbacombe
to view the sea
we went to Babbacombe
the family, and me.

We went to Babbacombe
to a village minute
we went to Babbacombe
model village, it's cute.

We went to Babbacombe
on a drizzly day
we went to Babbacombe
by a clifftop, railway.

We went to Babbacombe
the sun came out
we went to Babbacombe
ice cream, we shout.

We went to Babbacombe
a picnic with a view
we went to Babbacombe
it's beautiful, it's true.

View of the sea from Babbacombe Green.

Babbacombe Model Village.

Robert Worrall

Old Wardour Castle

Old Wardour Castle
damaged beyond repair
I can sense your sadness
I feel, your despair.

Built for Lord Lovel
during the 100 years war
in the 14th Century
your design, top drawer.

You're a castle unique
six sides, not four
with many guest rooms
a luxury, to adore.

You're just so beautiful
a castle luxurious
then came more troubles
civil war, notorious.

Roundheads took control
as the Baron was away
then came his son
who left you, in decay.

Damaged and hurt
yet still, you have a heart
you're a beautiful castle
a ruin, that's smart.

Old Wardour Castle.

Inside Old Wardour Castle.

Ochy Hole

Ochie Hole
it's a spooky cave
come see the witch
do you, feel brave.

Ochie Hole
of the Mendip Hills
when it rains
the River Axe, spills.

Ochie Hole
or the Okey Hole
a cave, cave, cave
for you, to stroll.

Ochie Hole
is a place of mystery
with lots to offer
ancient, history.

Ochie Hole
is a scientific dream
where horseshoe bats
in winter, teem.

A limestone cavern
with stalagmites to see
dare you explore
spooky cave, Wookey.

Wookey Hole Caves.

View from the platform.

Bratton Camp

On Bratton Down
near a horse of white
is Bratton Camp
upon a hill, of height.

Hidden from view
this castle of the past
Iron Age in date
forgotten, and passed.

It's the lesser known
of Westbury Hill
horse has visitors
but the camp, lies still.

It's an ancient place
with barrows too
three different types
of burials, but who?

I walked about
considering the past
who lived here
in this castle, so vast?

With only earthworks
banks and ditch
this place of mystery
long ago, was rich.

Bratton Camp Hill Fort.

Inside the earthworks.

Heatherslaw Railway

Heatherslaw railway
to Etal we go
by 15 inch gauge
it's slow, it's slow.

By steam we travel
on an engine in blue
it's name is Bunty
choo choo, choo choo.

It's about 4 miles
to Etal from the station
through pastures green
to our, destination.

Time passes slowly
photographs are taken
it's a wonderful trip
even though, I'm shaken.

Without any windows
a cool breeze fills the air
but it's really pleasant
not too much, it's fair.

Fifty minutes passed
and the castles in view
destination Etal
we've arrived, choo, choo.

Bunty.

Heatherslaw Railway.

Salisbury Cathedral

Cathedral church,
of Blessed Virgin Mary
a former name of a place,
now, legendary.

Salisbury Cathedral,
the name you're called
such a wonderful place
visitors, enthralled.

Built where an arrow fell
on an ancient ley
you're a place to adore
a place, to pray.

I came to visit
when the sun was bright
so many people
enjoying, your sight.

People having picnics
while others look inside
people being kind
so serene, and dignified.

Salisbury Cathedral
you're an artist's dream
a beautiful place
architecturally, supreme.

Salisbury Cathedral Cloisters.

Salisbury Cathedral.

I Walked Those Fields

I trekked the fields
through pastures green
the ley of the land
to Duddo circle, serene.

The sun was shining
birds singing in the trees
I walked those fields
there wasn't, any breeze.

The path went upwards
to the top of a hill
I walked these fields
to the stone circle, still.

I reached the summit
to the circle of mystery
without a doubt
this place, has history.

The circle I see
has some stones missing
yet still it's beautiful
our past's, reminiscing.

I trekked those fields
to the megaliths of stone
where I found a puzzle
from ancients, unknown.

Duddo Stone Circle

View across the fields from Duddo Stone Circle.

Tithe Barn

Your tithe must be paid
to the abbey near
a tenth of your income
each, and every year.

A portion of your wares
like corn or fleece
you must pay your tithe
your rent, your lease.

To the barn you go
where the tithe is stored
you must pay up
your tithe, your board.

This barns in Lacock
tithe barn for the abbey
now it's restored
as it was, a little shabby.

Built in the 14th Century
it's a barn with charm
no tithes now paid
no goods, from the farm.

Required tithes no more
yet this barn remains
it's now ancient history
my poem, explains.

Lacock Tithe Barn.

Mompesson House

Mompesson House
in Salisbury
was constructed for
Mompesson, MP.

Queen Anne in style
on Cathedral Close
it's a lovely building,
so grandiose.

'Twas an MP's home
and an artist's too
a Bishop's residence
a house, to view.

With its walled garden
you can relax in peace
after looking around,
this, masterpiece.

Sense and sensibility
was filmed here too
a period drama
on location, it's true.

Mompesson House
in Salisbury
it's the perfect place,
with history.

Mompesson House from the gardens.

Mompesson House (front).

Uley Long Barrow

Hetty Pegler's Tump
a Neolithic mound,
in the place of Uley
a long barrow, found.

Named after the wife
of a landowner past,
this gallery grave
had burials, amassed.

Excavations found
fifteen skeletons inside,
and a Roman intruder
of later date, who died.

I seem really nervous
as I enter within,
this cave of darkness
goose bumps, on skin.

I touch the walls
while I stumble about
this place is silent
no voices, that shout.

Reaching the back
I feel death all around,
I don't belong here
on this, sacred ground.

Uley Long Barrow.

Looking inside.

Silbury Hill

Silbury Hill, Silbury Hill
an ancient mound
built,
with skill.

Silbury Hill, Silbury Hill
40 metres high
an enigma,
to thrill.

Silbury Hill, Silbury Hill
by legend a burial
for a King,
called Sil.

Silbury Hill, Silbury Hill
in the Kennet valley
gives you,
a chill.

Silbury Hill, Silbury Hill
a true enigma
a Prehistoric,
hill.

Silbury Hill, Silbury Hill
an ancient puzzle
quiet,
and still.

Silbury Hill.

Silbury Hill from the roadside.

Robert Worrall

Sea Monster

Up the mini mountain
by tram we go
a chunk of limestone
from sea, on show.

Slowly, slowly
the tram moves on
stopping halfway
you catch, another one.

Right to the top
there's beauty to adore
pass ancient mines
of Bronze Age, I'm sure.

We're at the summit
it's windy up here
it doesn't really matter
it's lovely, I cheer.

Let's take a walk
there's so much to see
wildlife for one
such beauty, we agree.

Viking for sea monster
is what it means
Great Orme, Llandudno
beautiful, scenes.

The Great Orme from Llandudno Pier.

Great Orme Tram.

Genius of the Place

By the source of the Stour
an estate of grace
in the village of Stourton
Genius, of the Place.

For five hundred years
the Stourton's lived here
Barons of Stourton
a three baronies, peer.

This place has everything
woods and farms
gardens and mansion
and a lake, with charms.

Look out for the temples
and King Alfred's tower
the Iron Age hill forts
Rhododendrons, in flower.

Walk around the lake
find the Nymph of the Grot
the spirit of the spring
in this place, time forgot.

Stourhead Estate
is beauty, genius and art
it'll leave you amazed
and shall enter, your heart.

Stourhead.

The Gateway.

King Alfred's Tower.

The Gothic Cottage.

The Nymph of the Grot.

Temple of Apollo.

The bridge and the Pantheon.

Waterfall.

ROBERT WORRALL
(I'M JUST A MAD POET)

I'm just a mad poet
with a camera and pen
travelling around
writing poems, my zen.

Taking photos
of the things that I see
then giving information
in lines, of poetry.

I'm just a mad poet
with rhymes in my head
rambling all around
by verse, I'm led.

From historical places
to woods and hills
I'm following the verse
everything, thrills.

I'm just a mad poet
taking note of the lines
photographing places
the poetry, designs.

I can sense the voices
from the places I go
they all speak to me
but I'm mad, you know.

FIND ME ON FACEBOOK
A MAD POET'S RAMBLINGS

Made in the USA
Columbia, SC
27 June 2018